勇媽

Mothers Lead

Jenny Athena Wong

勇媽

Mothers Lead

Jenny Athena Wong

A Memoir

A Modern Woman

A Mission

一個女人的日記

The Journey of a Girl to Motherhood

The Power of Women to Advance Evolution

The Mission to Empower Women
Who Will In Turn
Elevate All

Table of Contents

HORSEPOWER

勇 Brave

媽 Mother

女 Woman

馬 Horse

A Mother Is A Brave Workhorse

Stronger Than All Men

Men Have Room For Improvement

Ladies and Gentlemen

You Are Perfect

I don't mean to be a bummer

If I am to tell a story about Life
It must start as a seed

Don't worry
It gets Happier

Simple Duty

I don't know much about my family history
Other than what my Mother tells me

I am told that my Grandfather was a Doctor
Trained in Chinese and Western Medicine

A Boy was gravely ill
My Grandfather saved him

The grateful Mother felt she owed her son's Life to him

She asked him to accept the boy as a godson
The boy would honor him as his own Father

Grandfather courteously declined
He simply fulfilled his daily duty

She begged relentlessly

He did not expect gains from the relationship
If it appeased the insistent mother

He accepted

Gossamer Veil

Communist Pretense

One night
Communists stormed the house

Looted Everything.

Money, furniture, clothes

Food.

Everything.

common thieves thinly veiled as revolutionaries

Overnight

My Mother was the
Daughter of a wealthy prestigious Family
Cast down to the very pit bottom of the new social order

Intellectuals attacked as
Bourgeois enemies of the Regime

Grandfather was a practicing Christian
Another Communist stone of sin

Subject to Violence, Humiliation, and Abject Poverty
Punished for Saving Lives
Persecuted for Faith in Humanity

I have read accounts of the social climate and the
Communists' rationale for revolution

I cannot condone it

How do Tyrants seize power?

RATIONALIZATION

To Destroy

Thousands of Years of Knowledge

Is Just Pure Bigotry

a toddler

throwing a tantrum

Life Begets Life

The young boy saved was now a
Young man working overseas

He sent as much money as
He could home to Grandfather

He Saved Our Family

He helped my uncle find work in America

After my uncle obtained citizenship
He sponsored our Family for immigration

Precious Sprout

At the Very Beginning of Life

I Escaped Death Twice

My grandmother had three daughters
Only one son

She felt a failure to ancestral duties if a
Male heir could not be produced to
Carry the family line

After my sister was born
They risked for a second child

Late into her pregnancy
Such that it was impossible to conceal

Mom stayed hidden

We Were Betrayed

A Guard Found My Mother

"You are in Violation of the One Child Policy

I am here for Standard Operating Procedures

Extraction and Tubal Ligation"

Mom begged.

"We will be immigrating to America
We are only waiting for our turn
We will all be gone soon

I will stay hidden
I will send the child away
I promise not to have more children

PLEASE

You can report you fulfilled your duty"

Mom was always Kind and Generous to Everyone

Well-liked in the Community

The Guard was Merciful

Once born
I was smuggled away as evidence of a crime

But Mom could not bear to be without her Child
Her Daughter

She wanted me home

To Register an Illegal Life as one of Permitted Statutory Existence

They paid a very heavy fine
Three times the average annual salary
A sum few can afford

Providentially
My parents ran a successful small business

I Was Worth It

Worthless Weed

Had I been born into any other family
My probability of survival was extremely low

"One Girl is not ideal, but perhaps acceptable
 A Second Girl is completely Useless!

WHAT !?!

I have to pay a heavy fine for her !?!
We don't have that kind of money

Even if we did
I wouldn't waste it on THAT"

No Mother would at the Birth of Her Child say

"It's a Girl
 I don't want it
 Here. Dispose of It"

Father is Executioner

Life ripped from Her bosom

She fights in vain
She has no power
She has no voice
She must obey

How do you conveniently dispose of a worthless baby girl?

Dumped in the river
Abandoned in the woods
Strangled

Murdered by the very Hands that Gave Her Life

She Arrived in the Wrong Packaging

Wild Child

My happiest memories of early childhood in China are of
Roaming freely around the village

I climbed the highest trees

Welcomed the silky caterpillar meandering onto my fingers
Admired the iridescent wings of the cicadas beetle buzzing on the
bark

Rustled the brush to rouse grasshoppers out of hiding
Kicks tickled as they fought to escape from my cupped hands

Leaned over the creek edge to grab clutches of fish eggs
Stalked dragonflies as they landed on a reed to rest

Scooped tadpoles to study their
Metamorphosis from waggy tails to legged frogs

Beheld water bugs dance
Sending out tiny rhythmic ripples across the placid lake surface

Later in adult life
I asked Mom

"How come you let me run around by myself like that?

Is that what people did back then?

Let kids run Wild?"

Mom retorted

"Of course not!
We had a nanny and grandma take care of you

You ran off all the time!!
You were there one moment, then gone in a flash

Your grandfather scolded me all the time!!

'Someone saw her playing at the lake by herself again

Get her under Control !!

She is going to Die !!! '"

Oh

I was not allowed to do any of that

My Young Instinct

Did Not Heed Prescribed Restrictions

I have a scar from stitches on the right side of my forehead
I have no recollection of how I got hurt

Mom says I hit a brick wall

Well, I didn't die that time

I must have been really frustrated to be
Banging my head on the wall like that

Rudimentary School

I entered first grade American public school
Not knowing a single alphabet

By third grade I was in the supposedly
Gifted and Talented Education Honors class at a

Not so good school in a
Not so good neighborhood

Still Rudimentary

I should still be Thankful

Subpar Education is Better than No Education

Marine Magic

With the exception of fourth grade Ms. Tweeney

Wild silver oceanic windblown hair

Adventure seeking Seamaiden sprinting up stony trails

Ebb Tide Exploration

Barefoot toes sink into shared sand with harbor seals absorbing
solar rays
Toddlers just as spirited as us

Limpets and barnacles decorate sandstone rocks like snowflake
sprinkles on caramel cake

Chocolate patched kelp crabs disappear sideward inside cracks and
crevices

Urchin pincushion boulder islands saturated with amethyst barbs

Periwinkle conoid spires nibble away on their sea lettuce barge

Sculpin fish dart through shallow pools under vegetation cover and
coastal rock camouflage

Mars dust moonglow anemones convulse in deep belly tickles by
the slightest touch

Tyrian sunflower stars streaked with magenta shift shape as they
slink away from curious wandering eyes

As we summit the crystalline iceplant embroidered cliff departing from our seascape excursion

We spot majestic whales across the mesmerizing aqua horizon dancing with ember fire

Magical

Pure Magic

Golden Sight

What I found lacking from my public school education
I supplemented with books from the public library

When school was not available
I developed my summers enveloped in the library catalog

Mountain chains of gleaming gold waiting to be gleaned

Collecting which books to borrow wasn't hard
Selecting which beyond the limit to leave behind was

As the capacity for the day was met
I locked up my bounty

Gleefully Happy
As I carried my heavy sack of treasure home

No way would I part from a single nugget

"Jenny. Put that book down. Go to sleep."
 Lights out.

Hmmph
I snuck reading under the covers by the night light

I had to start wearing glasses in fourth grade

Four eyes are better than Two

Oh Boy

I really loathed to be told

"Behave like a Girl"

WHAT !?!

I'm required to like dolls, speak softly and walk gently ?

I'm not allowed to like Transformers, Shout and Run !?!

Confined in Life
Adventurous in Thought

Nobody had Dominion

Charlie and the Chocolate Factory
Encyclopedia Brown
Fantastic Mr. Fox
Fudge-a-Mania
Narnia

Matilda and Pippi Longstocking were my kind of Girls

As long as I did not die in real life
Mom had no idea what kind of

Shenanigans I was up to in my head

Bare Necessities

If my eyes and a hand were free, there was a book
Even without hands, I managed to keep the pages open

When the urgency of nature called
I frantically ran through the house

Hunting for the precious spot
Where I last laid down my book

I could not bear to sit a few minutes idle

Desperate.

I grab the toothpaste.

"Active Ingredient: Stannous Fluoride 0.454%
 Purposes: Anticavity, Antigingivitis, Antisensitivity"

Ahhhhh . . . . . . relieved

Character School

I was doodling in my notebook
Started to write my name

I got stuck.

I forgot how to write my name properly

"Mom !!

I need to attend Chinese school !!"

Starting in third grade
Everyday after school

I studied for two hours at a
Taiwanese School in Chinatown for six years

The rigor of Chinese School was a
Required augment to my unsatisfactory public schooling

Two hours of daily instruction were
Far more than full days waiting in vapid classrooms

I Loved Chinese School
School as it is Meant to Be

A place where I could safely step into
My place as a star pupil

Every day begins with a
Concerted class bow
Respectful greeting to the teacher

Daily Life Lessons

Culture, History, Literature, Philosophy, Ethics

Poetry, Idioms, Parables, Ideals, Principles

Calligraphy was my favorite subject

Control, Grace and Concentration

Create elegant works of Art with every brush

Every Character Perfectly Balanced

Hypotheflies

We had no toys

We couldn't afford them

We never asked for them

I kept myself amused in other ways

I folded an origami crane with the
Body puffed up like a blimp

Hypothesis

If I stuff enough flies in
Collectively, they would float the crane

Experiment

I caught flies

It didn't work.

Findings

I was in second grade
Obviously, I hadn't taken physics yet

To Hypothesize is only half the fun

UC Biology

Summer following fifth grade
I opportunely attended the

GATEWAY Program for Gifted Students

A joint program with
UC Berkeley to study with real Professors

I selected Biology

I can still remember walking on campus

Red brick roads
Wild strawberry ground cover with tiny ruby berries speckled all
over
Squirrels lured off their oak tree with peanuts

Open lab with large glass windows and beakers
Long countertops that I rested my elbows on as
I cupped my face

Contently studying the Professor
Gleefully swinging my feet off the tall pedestal

Experiment

Identify an Ideal Fertilizer

I recalled back in the villages
Farmers just peed in the fields

Yup. Pee

Fast-acting source of
Nitrogen, Phosphorus and Potassium

Fresh urine is sterile and non-toxic
Older urine is quickly processed in compost

Compared to our agricultural practice of composting
Fecal matter

poop?

hmm

pee seems better

I can say with full honesty and in good humor

"I studied Biology at UC Berkeley when I was nine"

Down Down Down

When we first arrived in America
We shared a small two bedroom apartment
With my aunt's family

We moved for a place of our own
A tiny one bedroom in the
Basement of the same building

My parents thought

"We can't have our kids living in the basement forever
  This is no condition for them to study in"

They did everything they could to save for a down payment

Several years later

They bought the best house they could afford
Tucked in a tiny pocket neighborhood that was quiet

The surrounding area

Was Not

My assigned middle school and high school a few blocks
Down

Were the Worst in the City

Where Gang Fights, Abuse, Date Rape

Gun Violence

ARE REAL

I was required to enter that school
The fall following UC Berkeley

Teachers were mediocre
But they tried their best

Always tested wrangling rowdy kids
Barely getting most to catch up
Many were a lost cause

Kids took free education for granted

Disrespectful to teachers
Disruptive in class

They were mean

I couldn't advance my studies

I Hated It
I Absolutely Hated It

School Mates

Mom worked too much to possibly monitor us

She was deathly afraid we would
Fall into the wrong crowd

Given the terrible schools I attended
That was not an unfounded fear

A Lifelong Paranoia of Comrades
Required to report on neighbors, friends and family

Trust was Not an Asset that One Could Afford

A Lifetime of Ingrained Fear and Danger
Certainly did not put her at ease

Despite Us Being in a Safer Place Now

The only way she thought
She could keep us safe was to

Restrict social activities only to School

Coolest Ever

My only Saving Grace was my
Science Teacher

Michael J. Fox

Mr. Fox had a broad smile and long ponytail
Served in the Peace Corps

The Magician Who Dazzled Us with
Intricacies in the Science of Life

Mr. Fox was the COOLEST!!!

Professor Who

The Owl plinko ping pong ball pneumatic tube
Wise probability student participation selector

Kids Science Magazine

Lightning Thrill of Science Jeopardy

<u>Provoking Brain Tickles in My Research Reports</u>

Botulism

Potato Blight

Mad Cow Disease

Bacterial Decomposition

Dominion

Which Way Life Teeters Is Entirely Of

Our Own Making

Global Warming

Pollution

Extinction

Evolution

Ecosystem Detriments

GMO's

Monopolies

Invasive Species

Single Yield Crops

Chemical Fertilizers

Cross Pollination Contamination

Herbicide Insecticide Adaptive Resistance

Depletion

Extinction

Ethical Magic

Gene splicing

Cloning Dolly

Engineering Cool

Science Club Was Even Cooler!!

Gauged Tensile Strength

Erected pasta bridges across extended gaps

Building suspension as load after load was loaded onto
Unknown solidity

Demonstrated Aerodynamic Efficiency

Constructed balloon powered race cars

Launched down the prolonged hall
Outshooting land rockets one after another

Origami flights customized by strategic snips

Aerobatic plane performing
Acrobatic aerial maneuvers until it
Graced the gymnasium ground last place

Might I brag to say My Designs were Pretty Cool?

Starstruck

I LOVED

When Mr. Fox rolled in the television to show

Wacky Bill Nye

The Science Guy !!!

I LOVE COOL GUY NYE !!!!!!

If I practiced idolatry

Bill Nye would be right after Mr. Fox

. . . ok
   maybe before

Coolest World Ever

Life is Simple

Light Water Air Earth

Build the Perfect Sealed
Self-Sustaining Earth Cycle

I laid my materials on the table

Globe

Large plastic bottles, scissors, duct tape

Ocean

Water, aquatic plants, goldfish, water snails

Land

Soil, plants, snails from the yard

I left for a quick dinner
Couldn't have been gone for more than 15 minutes

When I came back, much to my dismay

I discovered that my fattest snail had run away!!!

I searched all over for him, slime trails help

Don't underestimate a snail

Formed In One Night

Sun   Ocean   Sky   Earth

My Perfect Biosphere

Sat by the warm classroom window all semester

Creator proud that my goldfish and snails

Lived happily in their

Own Little World

I could blab on and on . . .

You get the gist

SCIENCE IS THE COOLEST !!!!!

Heavy

To Share Burden Is To Be
Grateful For What Burden Grants

Mom taught how to select produce throughout Chinatown

Knock on a watermelon
The thud will tell you its sugar content

Two oranges identical in appearance, toss in your hand
The heavy one is plump and juicy, light one hollow and dry

When the bags became too many
Mom stationed me in front of the photo shop as
She continued to travel shop to shop seeking the best prices

Whiling guarding the bags
I watched through the glass

Other families' happy holiday memories
Released one after another

Walking our full load to the train station

Bags so heavy
The plastic straps dug into my fingers

I'd stop for a moment
Readjust the straps to a different part of my arm

Mom turned back

"Are you ok, Jenny?
Is it too heavy?
Here, give me some to carry"

I stand straight.
Step forward.

"No, Mom
I can carry more"

Power Work

As we shaped dumplings for the week

Mom instructed

"One day you will have a Family of your own
   You need to know how to run a household

   A Girl needs to know how to cook and clean
   I'm making you do this for your own good"

"Mom

   I'm going to be a Power Woman
   By the time I have a family, I can hire help"

She laughed

"We'll see"

Damned Work

I absolutely abhor chores, banal housework
Sisyphus' Eternal Torture

Persistent fellow that he is
The guy deserves a break too

God be my witness
I'm pushing that Damned rock off the cliff

Workflow

I see Family and Work as more of an Ebb and Flow

Sometimes You are Pulled from one side to another
Sometimes You Swim
Sometimes You Float

Always reach for a Life Saver when you spot one

You don't have to be perfectly balanced at all times

Go With the Flow

Don't Sink

Done

My Uncle asked Mom to work at his restaurant

She worked a lot and asked for little pay in return
She was already so grateful to him for sponsoring us

"He is the only reason
 You can pursue an Education here"

Mom never let me forget that

She asked whether I could help her if I had free time

So on weekends and holidays
I helped her as best I could

I scraped people's uneaten food into the trash
Loaded dishes into the industrial washer
Mopped bathrooms

Deshelled blocks of defrosted shrimp
Wrapped trays of wontons and egg rolls
Stuffed and shaped potstickers
Cut onions

Prepped ingredients for mom to cook
One dish after another with no down time

Tossed in the heavy wok over
Roaring orange flames and blue sparkles

Something I did was
Something Mom didn't have to

Done

When David was born
We had more family to take care of him

By the time I entered high school
I was the only one left

Every morning
I took him to school on the train
Walked down the hill to attend class

Every afternoon
I walked up the hill
Took him home on the train

When mom came home at 9pm
David was fed, bathed, in bed
Dishes done, laundry hung

Feed Knowledge

My parents ran the restaurant for a few years
Which was just down the street from a Community College

Costs has risen, but their prices did not

"Mom
  You need to keep up with expenses
  Increase your prices"

She shushed me.

"These are College Students, Poor Scholars

  Many international students with
  No Family to take care of them

  Give them a good meal
  Let them focus on their studies"

"To Earn Enough is Enough"

Lowell High Scholars

I earned admission to Lowell High School

A Magnet Alternative Public School for
Students with high GPA and standardized test scores

San Francisco's Cream of the Crop Young Minds

Campus ran like a University
Courses were University level

Finally.
School in its Proper Order

I dare not even fathom how Life would have turned out

If I was forced to attend my assigned school

only bleak.

Better Than Whom

First Day of School

Mom said

"These Kids come from good families
  They went to better schools

  You have to work harder to catch up"

I know she only said that to motivate me

It did the Opposite.

To tell your Child
They are not as good as Someone else

Does more Harm than good

She got it in my head that the
Other Kids were Better than me

Parenting 101

Use Positive Statements

"These Kids come from good families
  Attended good schools

  Work Hard.
  You Are Just As Good"

Same intent spoken differently

Yields entirely different results

JROTC

Military Training is Unparalleled

Impeccable Standards

Leadership	Integrity	Service
Discipline	Courage	Honor
Character	Respect	Duty

Classic poster on the Company wall
"Shoot for the Moon"

OUR POTENTIAL

SHOOTS INFINITELY BEYOND

Drill Platoon

Every Command Executed in Perfect Synchronicity

SHARP

CRISP

BEAUTIFUL

Reflection

Bridget

We competed for cadet of the month
First mistake.

She was better than me at everything
Faster. Stronger. Smarter.

Beautiful. Confident. Sharp.

Tough.

Boys Drill Team

See?
I told you She's Cool

We both had aspirations for Medical School
Younger Brothers to mentor

She didn't always have to listen to her parents

They catered to her every whim
Piano, gymnastics, art

Her parents paid for an expensive SAT prep course
I bought a book to study alone

Same score

Bridget Rode Through Life with Confidence and Ease

Did What She Wanted
Confirmed in Her Choices

If it was wrong
She just laughed it off

"Oops. Whatever"

Best Friends

So much alike
Yet so different

How I wished I could be her

Me

Footsteps

Every Person has their path

As much as I wished that ours was the same

I have to walk my own

It is not mine alone

Diss the Mold

I had been trained to behave exactly as I was told
"A Good Girl"

Makes for a well-behaved Child
Stifles an Independent Will

As Responsibilities grow
The Self shrinks

The faster you morph into your assigned societal role
The greater amplified pressure the mold compresses in

An ornate kimono
Ever-adapting kabuki mask

I miss the unfettered days of my

Wild younger self ruling the landscape

Freedom to wander where I wished

Liberty to grasp the off limits

TOTAL DISREGARD OF EXPECTATIONS

time spent cocooned in an
ornate silk kimono has its lessons learned

unassuming grace and charm work wonders

a right time and place for every face

Kiss the Frog

Prom

Henry's hands trembled as
He wrapped his arms around me for photos against a backdrop of
morning sky

He's probably had a crush on me
Since the third grade in Chinese school

Sorry, Henry

I don't mean to embarrass you

You are the Hero Nerd who got the Girl

When he finally worked up the courage to ask her out

Nine years later

Oh, wait

Now that I recall

You didn't ask me out personally

You went through Marie

I guess an intermediary still counts ???

Ladies

Lock down a Nerd
A Nerd is Earnest and Honest

Like a fine wine cooler

He generally does a lot better after high school
Than the Cool Boys

You can easily swap his glasses out for contacts
Refresh his wardrobe

You Kissed the Frog

Now He's a Prince

Nerds

Sorry for calling You the Frog from Science lab

I couldn't think of a better analogy

This One's Perfect

Now Listen Up Gentlemen-in-training
Now that I helped You Get the Girl

Treat Her Right
Show You Deserve Her

Don't Start to Act Smug

NO GAMES.

I Will Overturn My Stellar Review
If I See that Happen

Don't Ruin It For Everyone Else

GOT IT?

Good.

Jocks, Bad Boys, and Handsome Devils

Keep Up With The Nerds

SMART IS SEXY

Literary Life

Thank You

Ms. Bookwalter

Before You
I had only been taught to
Consume and regurgitate information

Book Altar Lessons
Capture Wisdom Created From Atmospheric Thin Air

Beyond
What Surrounds Us, Of How

I didn't know I had captured thought to express

Well, to be fair
I've never had more than an audience of one

You were the Second

Persuasive Writing and Oratory Power

Athena
Warrior Goddess of Wisdom and Justice

Shakespeare
Artful Plays and Soulful Sonnets

Molière
Hypocrisy and Honesty

Odyssey
Journey

Ms. Bookwalter

I only exist in words
Because of You

I am forever grateful

Feel
Not Tell

Thank You

Ms. Canepa

For showing Shakespeare as it was meant to be

All the hidden jabs and naughty bits
Wit of primary secondary tertiary language

I Love How You

Cackled with laughter as the words appeared
Barely able to catch your breath as you tried to explain

Thank You

For painting portraits of flesh and blood people from
Nectar in a Sieve

A beautifully sad story
A fictional tale far too real

I hope my tale wins them Freedom and Strength

Ms. Canepa

I only exist in words
Because of You

I am forever grateful

Midsing Chemistry

Lysander and Hermia
Max and Jenny

We were madly in love in dialogue
I didn't speak to him off script

I was shy with boys

In an attempt to spark chemistry
Ms. Bookwalter tied our hands together

I still didn't talk to him.

There Max awkwardly sat.

As I ignored him to complete
Chemistry homework with my free hand

Ending Up

Opening Night

"Sleep well, My Love"

"Sleep well, Lysander"

An appropriately timed long kiss

Enthused Oohing and whistling
As one would expect from an audience of teenagers

then Puck popped up and messed everything up.

Through a Comedy of Errors

Everyone Ended Up

Happily Ever After

Understand

Backstage

Throngs of friends and family gushed praise and applause
I cut through the exuberant crowd of fans and flowers

My parents were not there.

They worked six days a week just to provide the basics
No way could they ask for time off to watch a silly play
Nor could they understand any of it

They were almost never at events.

No poetry contests, no cultural dances, no parades
No drama competitions, no Shakespeare, no Molière
No 91st competitions, no parent teacher conferences
No science fairs

No one waited for me.

as sad as I was to walk down the hall and out the school

silently crying alone

I understood

Better Than Whom

With testing and college applications
Coming around the corner

I said to Mom more often

"Sorry, I can't help you
 I have to study"

That semester
I earned a 4.15 GPA with
Advanced Placement Economics and Chemistry

Ironically
I got an 89 B+ in Chinese 7
I didn't have enough time to complete all my homework

I was Better than Most Kids

Quiet Work

Besides seeing my little brother tag along at
Rehearsals, company and drill platoon practice

No one had any idea the full extent of my responsibilities

I've been rather adept at putting on
A smile for everyone else

All My Life

Duty

I was a Group Leader for a

Bilingual Summer Program in Chinatown
An affordable option when public school was not available

Morning Academics

Afternoon Recreation

Field Trips and Camp

Most Parents, like mine

Were robbed of a proper education living through the
Cultural Revolution in Communist China

They worked harder than ever to offer their Children the
Opportunity to Earn a Better Life in America

Beyond that
They had limited insight to offer for
Success in this New World

Parents did their Best
We helped with the Rest

It Is My Duty To Be

The Bridge Over the Gap of Their World to Ours

This has always been My Life's Intention

Not Alone

At recess, while kids played with a flurry of activity

I saw my brother trace along the yard's perimeter

Hands on the straps of his backpack
Head down as if he didn't know what to do

All he managed was to shuffle his feet as
He stared at his shoes

He didn't know how to play

Worse than being socially awkward

he was alone

It pained me to see him lonely and lost
I held back my tears in public

I took off his backpack, excess weight

Guided him to a group of kids
Asked whether he could join in

They were glad to add a playmate

I knew I could not go far for college
I could not leave David behind

He could not stand steadfastly alone as I did

I did not want to see him crumble

Never Know

In the final hours of the
University of California System application deadline

I sat petrified before the computer.

an innocuous piece of paper
delivered in a plain envelope

Would Announce My Worth

Mom said

I was not as good as the other kids
If I didn't get good grades
I wouldn't get into a good school

I thought my GPA impressiveness for Berkeley lackluster
Any other UC was too far

How could I possibly think I would get into Stanford either?

I wasn't amongst our Sixteen Valedictorians

I wasn't perfect

therefore, I was not good enough

I let the night lapse
The window closed

I would not be told that
I was not good enough

Nor would I ever know whether

I WAS

Exactly Know

If I had shared this story that I'm telling you now
It would have weighed heavily in my application

I did not write these words.

I felt embarrassed for the work I had to quietly perform

I wasn't like the other kids

I was different

I Recognize Then

More Clearly Now

As Strength of Character

I Am Different

I AM EXACTLY

WHO YOU WANT

World Peace

Days before graduation
We gathered in the auditorium

Each Student was handed a slip of paper

The Principal Asked Us to
Contemplate Our Purpose in this Life

We Are About to Join
The Greater World As Citizens and Scholars

Decades from now
You will grasp this slip again

Did You Live Out Your Purpose?

Only Step

An ROTC Military Scholarship

Was the only way I could afford a
Top Nursing program at a private university

I didn't tell my parents that I had applied
Only informed them that I had accepted

I came home to a table of my parents and sister
A stern talk to tell me

"The Military is No Place for a Girl !!!!!

Why would You possibly want to do a thing

LIKE THAT !!?!!"

What could I say?

That I didn't trust to leave David in your hands?
That I was too worried to leave?

All I said

"This is what I want to do"

University of Self-Fulfillment

University of San Francisco

Jesuit Values

Educating Hearts and Minds to Change the World

Ethics
Philosophy
Theology

HOW TO THINK

NOT WHAT TO THINK

Perfectly Me

Finally Free to Focus on Myself

I was out to Prove I was Perfect

I took the Maximum Units allowed in a Semester

A+ Military Leadership

A+ Human Anatomy

A Great Philosophical Questions

A Advanced Written Communication

A Statistical Reasoning

A Military Fitness

Anatomy Ranked #1

Philosophy Professor Fr Anselm Ramelow invited me to his priesthood ordination

Writing Professor used my papers as teaching material

I Was Perfect

I WAS ALWAYS PERFECT

Ok, full confession

I wasn't perfectly perfect

I Missed the Military Physical Training Score

100 Maxed-out Push-ups

100 Maxed-out Sit-ups

 98 Run - 2 Points, 12 seconds shy of perfect

I'm still sore I missed those 2 points

I will continue to be sore until I train and hit 300

Either way

I'm going to be sore

Destined Moment

His Holiness the Dalai Lama Tenzin Gyatso was
Coming to speak at our Cathedral

I coveted a golden ticket

I settled in at the adjacent Library
My second home

Hardly able to contain myself
Waiting for the anticipated hour

I started a paper to stay occupied

Ironically

Deep in thought writing my Philosophy paper

I lost track of time

missed the golden moment

Perhaps We Were
Not Destined to Meet Then

For I would have only looked on Him with
Awe from the audience

Today

Well

That's a Different Story

Tough Like A Girl

Boot Camp

Blindfolded dive, Rifle overhead treading water

Fully loaded rucksack, Solid combat boots

Obstacle courses, STX Lanes

Rope courses, Repelling

Land navigation, Fire watch

Humvee

HOOOO-RRRRRAAAAAHHHH!!!!!

I LOVED IT

I Wasn't Told To Behave Like A Girl

I AM JUST AS TOUGH AS

THE NEXT GUY

Hold Your Instrument

Marksmanship is a Discipline of Control

Control of Your Instrument.
Your Body. Your Heartbeat. Your Breath.

Position set. Sight set.
Breathe in, breathe out
gentle tap

Three shots.
One spot.

In JROTC

We used air rifles with tiny pellets
Aimed at one inch concentric circles

The worst harm would be a tiny bruise

In this Moment

My Instrument.
M16 Assault Rifle

My Sight.
Trained on a Human Silhouette
Target Centered on His Chest

This was No Longer Marksmanship

I Enlisted to Save
I was being Trained to Kill

Reality Hit Me.

Don't Shoot.
Put Our People at Risk

Refuse to Shoot.
Insubordination
Court martial offense
Dishonorable discharge

Shoot.
How could I ever forget his face as
Life drained from his eyes?

A Horror Far Too Many Souls
Battle to the End of Days

2003

The likelihood that I would be a
Soldier First was Escalating

The Sergeant's words rang in my head

"You Are A Soldier First"

I closed my eyes.
Pulled the trigger.

I didn't care where the bullet hit

I CANNOT DECIDE DEATH

WEAPON

Back on campus we learned how to clean our weapons

To disassemble and reassemble with
Surgical precision and speed

I stopped paying attention
This was one lesson I thought I'd never need

Pretended I didn't know what I was doing
Asked the Corporal to "show me how it's done"

I Withdrew From My Military Scholarship

My Weapon of Choice

WORDS

I HONE EVERY MOMENT

Not Me

Something had upset me
I could not sleep

Next day in class
I was tired and distraught

I couldn't think
I couldn't concentrate

Suddenly gripped with intense anxiety
I escaped to the restroom

I couldn't breathe
I couldn't stop crying

I doubled over in pain as
My body spasmed uncontrollably on the cold hard tiles

My first panic attack

Quit Being Happy

I chose to study Nursing
In preparation for Medical School

Not a common selection for
Aspiring doctors with the need to impress

It is Vital to

Treat Patients and Families as People

Not just physiological pathology puzzles

A Tragic Story was in the news

A Nurse had killed an infant by mistake

She administered an adult dosage
The vials looked so much alike

Medical mistakes happen
More often than you'd like to know

I could easily be that Nurse

My patients could not afford for me
To have a bad day

Not a single bad moment

Unintentional Death is still Death

Hippocratic Oath

"First, Do No Harm"

I couldn't guarantee I could live up to that

The burden of taking care of everyone else first had
Taken its toll

I had little strength left for me now

I had No One
Nothing to fall back on

The One Certainty
I've Held My Whole Life

I could not be

I transferred to the School of Business

I was never really quite happy after that

Not So Smart

I graduated with Majors in
Finance, Accounting, and Hospitality Industry Management

I joined a Public Accounting Firm

The Banks Failed.

Even as Embers Smoldered

From the Last Firestorm

Ignited by Arrogance and Fueled by Fraud

WE LEARNED NOTHING

People Who Think They Are

The Smartest In The Room

Are The

DUMBEST

Arrogance is Ignorance

Protect Whom

After yet another Global Financial Collapse
Was I naive to think Auditors would take to heart

"Protector of the Capital Market"?

It seemed they were there to
Make partner or land the next cushy job

The Firm itself is a for-profit model

Footsteps

When David was in high school
I came home to find him in a JROTC dress uniform

You know your little brother looks up to you when
He Follows in Your Footsteps

I was Proud of this Young Man

Proud he made a Commitment to
Develop Character necessary to be

A Global Citizen
A Gentleman

Secure In A Battalion We Could Trust

Self-Serving Sunshine

The following year
I asked David how he was progressing in JROTC

He informed me that the

San Francisco School Board had
Shut down the program

fools

San Francisco

You Are My Hometown

You Are Distinctive

Your Free Spirit To

Accept People As They Are

Your Warrior Spirit To

Fight For Fairness

Yet Some San Franciscans can be
Far Too Liberal to a Detriment

Your short-sighted policies hurt the very People whom
You claim you aim to serve

Even as Students protested and cried tears that
You were Dismantling Their Family

You beamed with pride at
Your false self-righteousness

You. Don't. Care.

You Only Care to Broadcast Your Agenda

Brag of Your Moral Superiority

Fortunately

Truly Righteous People Overturned Your Folly

Reinstated JROTC several years later

TOO LATE FOR TOO MANY

In Your blind attempt to curb Military Recruitment
You Fed Recruits to Gangs and Criminals

You Eliminated the
Best Chance a Child with a Rough Life
Could have Any Chance at Life

You Ousted Them From the
Only Family They Could Count On

You Kicked Their Face into a Muddy Road of
Lifetime Underachievement

WHY DON'T YOU

BRAG ABOUT THAT?

Self-Centered

We Have Enjoyed
Unprecedented Peace and Prosperity
Since We Won World War II

Any War After Was Fought Outside Our Borders

The One Time We Were Attacked Within

You curled up comfortably on your couch
Sipping a cup of chamomile tea
Nonchalantly watching it
Collapse on television

Oh, gosh
That must of been so traumatic for you

Our Apologies
We blocked your Chi, inconvenienced you

WE WON'T

LET IT HAPPEN AGAIN

go on

bounce along blissfully Ignorant without a blip

Center Yourself

Focus on Yourself

Balance Your Chi Again

because all that really ever matters in this Life is

how fuzzy You feel

You are the Center of the Universe

Self-Loving Ingrate

Do You Really Think What Keeps You Safe

is your
good karma, positive vibes and happy thoughts?

Servicemen Do Not Start Wars

Take It Up With True Instigators

DO NOT INSULT
Ladies and Gentlemen

Who Risk Their Lives
To keep you safe in your cozy little one

Their Families Compromise
For yours to play

YOU ARE UNGRATEFUL

Tread Lightly

Military Training is Unparalleled

Impeccable Standards

Leadership   Integrity   Service

Discipline   Courage   Honor

Character   Respect   Duty

I wish I had graduated as
2nd Lieutenant Commissioned Officer
STARDOM

Military Training should be offered for Everyone
Whether You join the ranks formally
Or engage in combat is

YOUR DECISION

To Shoot Yourself in the Foot

Is to Broadcast a Glaring White Flag

To Invite Conflict and Violence

IF THEY COULD TAKE US OUT

THEY WOULD

The Greater Your Military Strength

The Less Likely Will You Need It

At Times

War is Necessitated to Save People from Cruelty

Particular Instigators Cannot Be Reasoned With

A Last Resort Is A Last Resort

A Nation of Trained Civilian Step Up

If You Are To Use It

GET IT RIGHT

march softly

Ask and You Shall Receive

I didn't ask for much help

"Who am I to anyone?
  Why would they take an interest in me?"

I Sought Wisdom from My Secret Council on the Shelf

Paging Dr. Wong

David is a quiet conscientious person
Always willing to help

I'd find him studying in between restaurant tasks

"Mom
  Stop making him work at the restaurant

  He needs friends
  Let him go have fun

  He's wasting time here
  He needs to be a well-rounded candidate"

I checked on his progress

"David
 What are you up to?"

"Red Cross Club, Hospital Volunteer, Tutoring Kids

 Research Lab, Teaching Assistant

 Community Service Missioned Fraternity"

"Good.

 Keep it up"

David has a Kind Heart

A Good Head on His Shoulders

That's All A Mother Could Ever Ask For

When time came for interviews
I bought him a new suit, dress shoes

Dispensed final Motherly advice

"Tall Posture. Firm Handshake. Eye Contact.

Calmly share your thoughts
There is no reason to be nervous
They invited you to interview for good reason

You Belong"

David was a finalist for a full scholarship to UC Berkeley

Published Scientist at UC San Francisco

PharmD at UC San Diego

At least one of us is now

"Dr. Wong"

Belonging

I recall the day that my dad and I helped
David move into the dorms

As we were unpacking
Three freshmen came to the door to introduce themselves

We chatted for a few minutes
Then they asked me

"Hey, do you want to hang out?"

I laughed.

Flattered to be mistaken for a freshman
Glad to know my moisturizer and sunscreen are working

"My brother is the one moving in
 I'm seven years older than him"

Motioned to David
"Come, introduce yourself"

He shyly walked over to meet his first college mates

Longing

I already missed David as my dad and I
Walked back to the car

I took one last lingering look at campus
The place I wanted to be so many years ago

David is where he Belongs
I was happy about that

I felt lighter leaving

Happiness

To Gift Happiness Magnifies Your Own

We didn't have much
Yet Mom always gave

Never go empty handed
A gift received requires a gift in return

Any visit was precipitated by days of preparation
A matter of pride to be tasty and in perfect presentation

Packages of dumplings, steamed buns, sweet potato mochi
Bamboo leaf wrapped sticky rice

Meticulously inspected each piece of consideration

Selecting only the best to gift
Putting aside the misshapen for us

Mom always gave us fresh food first
Ate the leftovers herself

Always Gifts the Best

Reserves little for herself

It is no great wonder as to

Why the Guard spared my Life

Selflessness   Service   Sacrifice

I learned from Mom

HAPPINESS IS

TO GIFT HAPPINESS

no other way to live

New Hope

To Comfort Always

To Relieve Often

To Save Sometimes

Founded by Dr. Joyce and Robin Hill

Christians Who Dedicated Their Life's Purpose

To Care for Abandoned Children in China

Precious Sprouts

Healed, Fostered, Nurtured

Children receive the best medical care possible

Gentle souls preparing for passage receive palliative care

Carried by a full family in a warm tender home

FOREVER LOVED

Black Star

Allowed only One Child

You want the Perfect One

A DEFECTIVE OBJECT IS DISCARDED

For conditions as minor as a cosmetic cleft lip

Even if Parents desperately want to keep their Life

Despairingly
They could never afford the medical expense

Steeped in Superstition

The Stigma of a defective child lingers

"A Child Born of Misfortune Will Bring Misfortune"

"A BLACK STAR"

even then

A Perfectly Healed Child
Who Was Not Born Perfect

is still not good enough

Carried for Life

Mothers travel from afar
Carrying her Life

In Hopes they would have a better
Life with Someone Else

at the gate

she cradles her Love

for the last time

she kisses her Love

for the last time

carefully laid down

she steps back

her Life on the ground

she tearfully leaves carrying a

Lifelong Regret

Star Reborn

Children Usually Fulfill Their
Mother's Hope for a Better Life

Adopted by

Families Abroad Who Value Them
Families Who Cherish Them

from tragedy sprouts hope

Life Reborn with New Hope

Hang On

Mary

Her spinal fluid was leaking
She would not stay with us for long

We tried our best to keep her comfortable
Which was not always achievable

She cried through the night
I walked down in the darkness to soothe her

All I could do was look into her eyes
Hum, as her miniature fingers hung on mine

Seconds Count

Shelley

A tiny little soul due to her congenital heart defect
All skull, little body, light as a feather

One surgeon decided she was inoperable

We sought a second opinion
The Second Surgeon advised

"We can save her
 Book her surgery as soon as possible

 Hurry
 She does not have much time"

Time Ticks

A few weeks later

After I returned from my duties in Hong Kong
I cheerfully revisited everyone in the office

Casually asked
"How is Shelley? How was her surgery?"

The room grew quiet.

"Shelley left us a few days before her scheduled surgery"

I stood there and cried.

we were just a few days late

far too late

Simple Life

After kids laid down for their post-meal nap

I stepped into the empty cafeteria
Peacefully ate my modest meal

Stepped out to the vegetable garden

Breathing in same air
As lines of colorful clothing fluttering in the gentle wind

Sweet Simplicity

Afternoon stroll

Wheels, little shoes, firm soles

Clear skies, bright sun, warm breeze

We stopped for a surprise round of ice cream treats

Handed each Child exactly the
Same sweets as I had savored at their wee age

All Yours

One-on-one bicycle rides to the small village square

Uncontainable giggles
As we picked up speed on the dirt road

Emerald fields with nothing but
Sapphire skies above

Chive egg filled dumplings
Spun honey lollies
Grapes, lychees, longan

For one little afternoon
He didn't have to share

I was All His

Zoology

We chartered a bus for the Zoo
Singing and giggles the whole way

Bright-eyed faces pressed against the glass
Seeing these animals for the first time

We crossed the bridge over a serene lotus pond

Beauty Sprouted From Muck

Ying Yang

Pandas
The most playful creatures on earth

Open enclosure allowing us a
Glimpse into their world

Climbing, swinging, tumbling

When they retreated into the
Privacy of their backstage cubbies

We chanted

"回来, 熊猫! 回来!"

"Come back, Panda! Come back!"

Adorable ying yang fluffs made their

Encore appearance

"Yay!!!"

Winners

We stopped for dinner before heading home

Curious about an eclectic
Collection of kids and nannies

The manager inquired

I told him about New Hope

He returned with a load of meal prizes
Each Winner cheerfully picked their favorite

What a Kind Way to End the Day

We were all quite tired
When we got home after dark

Tired after a full day of play is the

GOOD KIND

The Good Side

Ben
A Clever Boy
A Clever Clever Little Boy

He figured everything out right away

He Could Read People

One afternoon

Ben pushed a little girl
Snatched the toy from her hands

I walked over immediately
Took the toy back

"That's not how you play
    Go say 'You're sorry'"

He crossed his arms.
Pouted.

Stared at me.

I could see the gears turning in his head

"Well, that didn't get me what I wanted"

click.

He threw open his arms
Huge grin

Ran to the girl
Gave her a big bear hug

"I'm sorry"

His eyes trained on me.

To tell me

"See?
I'm a good boy

Can I have what I want now?"

If he was wandering the streets lost and alone

A Predator would snatch its Prey
Turn him into a Monster

Blessedly
Ben was safe within his home at New Hope

Keep Your Eye on this One

Which Side He's On
Makes A Big Difference

Small Deed
Big Words

I assumed legal guardianship to take
Holly to Hong Kong for treatment

I was her Mother
She was my little Girl

My girl had a large lymphangioma mass on her left arm

MRI revealed abnormal lymphatic growth integrated throughout
her muscular and vascular tissue

Surgery would be too much for her little body to sustain
She would lose too much blood

Biopsy confirmed the tumor was benign

We could safely postpone surgery until she grows older and
stronger

Perhaps when she turns five

Other than a manageable physical impediment
The mass did not adversely affect other functions

Holly was Perfectly Healthy

MedArt's Surgeon summarized her report

"Eligible for Adoption"

Three short weeks

Three Big Words

"ELIGIBLE FOR ADOPTION"

A few months later
I received a simple email from New Hope

A photograph

Holly in an embroidered red and gold silk dress
Embraced by a lady with kind eyes and a warm smile

My little Girl has a Mother of her own now

Purely Happy

I love moments

When I entered the nursery
A clutch of Children rush to hug me

" 姐姐 !!"

" Big Sister !!"

I was happy

I was happy again

I was purely happy

after two months with New Hope

I returned home to the numbness of an empty Life

Wrong

The church overflowed
We had to sit in the aisles

She was a year behind me at Lowell
Huge grin, bubbly, energetic
Always promoting one cause or another

She graduated from Stanford
Was serving in the Peace Corps
Fighting for Women's Rights

she died there.

A Girl

So Beautiful, So Bright, So Full of Life

With the Desire to Change this World and the Power to Do So

she suddenly died.

it was wrong.

it was just wrong.

Existentialism

what have I done with my Life?

nothing.

what would people be able to say about me

if I died tomorrow?

not much.

Carbon Monoxide

I barely made it through work the next day

After most colleagues had left
I couldn't hold it anymore

I escaped into a private office to quietly cry

Then I couldn't stop
I began to sob
I couldn't breathe

I was having a panic attack

I gasped for air
Desperately trying to reclaim control

My Psyche told the Body

"She's been living a Life of comfort
She forgot our Purpose long ago

Jolt her !!
Wake her up !!!"

I wasn't in control anymore

My partner Wendy
Found me hyperventilating
Sobbing loudly on the floor

She helped me
Kindly guided me to her office
Gave me a big long hug

I stopped crying
I could breathe again

She called a friend to pick me up

There I sat. Dazed.

Half embarrassed. Half dazed.

the panic attacks became more frequent and intense

"NO"

"You Cannot Keep Lying To Yourself"

that chapter had to close

Adrift

I drifted

Pondered graduate school
Everything cost too much
Nothing was quite right

All I Truly Wanted Was Medical School

Same as before
I had neither the finances
Nor the support to safely assure success

To Volunteer was a way to Help without
Paying exorbitantly out of pocket

All You Ever Need

My parents worried about me
They worried I wouldn't be able to take care of myself

"You can't live off Volunteering

  Why do you keep Helping People?

  Why don't you help Yourself?"

they need me

I go where I'm needed

I wasn't driven to make money

When I tried to make money
I was never really quite happy

I fooled myself
Good company, good title, good pay

Ever Empty External Factors That
Will Never Last

Quench

Chinese Community Health Resource Center
In the same Chinatown hospital where David was born

The grounds where I grew up
I was now grown to water the earth

I searched through databases for grants
Prepared educational materials
Stationed at their tiny library

They were about to open a Spanish and Chinese Clinic
In the Worst part of the City

People Who Thirst For Them Most

Still Standing

Suicide Prevention and Crisis Line

To assure the terrified Schizophrenic
The figure at her window was not real

The Veteran who could not stop
Events looping through his mind

The Mother who blames herself for her
Adult Child's Lifelong struggle for lack of prenatal care

The Man who wanted to walk into the woods
Never look back

He called back to thank me

The Woman who wanted to jump

We kept Life linked on the line until a
Friend promised to take her home

Not Leave Her Alone

A Young Man called
"I'm hungry
 How can I get something to eat?"

It was late at night, all the soup kitchens had closed
I checked the schedule to see whether there
Might be a slim chance

there wasn't.

"They were giving sandwiches at the park
 . . . three hours ago

            I don't know whether there's anything left now"

. . . that felt like a white lie of yearning hope

     I felt useless
         completely useless
             words cannot quiet a hungry stomach

Always wrap with
"How are You going to take care of Yourself?"

"Warm bath. Hot tea
 Go to sleep"

"Good. Goodnight
 Call back tomorrow if you need to"

I wished they wouldn't

Coming home at 11pm after a shift

Mom's ginseng chicken soup
Warmed on the table
Waiting for me

Those Were Good Nights

Words
Simple little words

Enough to bring
Life back from the brink

More steps back
Fewer steps forward

Sometimes
To stand still is good enough

Wait

She was at the tail end of terminal cancer

Nothing more they could do for her now
Only try to keep her comfortable

Her husband just needed someone to
Sit with her while he went grocery shopping

So she would not be alone

I told him to take his time
Sat beside her bed

Every once in a while
Asked whether she needed anything

She smiled and slightly shook her head
A few times took a sip of water

As we waited
I admired the photos on her wall

An expansive family that required professional photography and
extra large print to capture

Her husband returned with heavy groceries
Profusely apologized for taking so long

I assured him it wasn't

I left feeling as if I had just witnessed

The Ultimate Romance

Boy meets Girl
Boy falls for Girl
Love, Marriage
Kids, Grandkids

A Lifetime Together
Now Old Man and Old Woman

If I would be so lucky as to have my old man hold my hand
As I prepare to leave this world

Then I hold out my hand

Wait

True Love

True Love is Full of Shit.

Meet Cute. Perfect Match. Soulmate.

Bullshit.

Beautiful and Accomplished

Men Desire You, Chase You
A trophy to lord over lesser men

Easy to love
Easy to believe this love is real

Ephemeral essence can evaporate any moment

Marred Beauty and Bereft Intellect
Who are You?

What is Your worth to Him now?

Life Happens.
Shit Happens.

When You fall ass first into the Abyss
Will He dive to catch You?

Maybe

Maybe Not

From the Very Beginning of Life to the Very End

We All Need Someone To

Wipe Our Ass

Only People Who

Truly Love You Are Willing

TRUE LOVE IS

FULL OF SHIT.

Useful

I had three weeks of vacation with
No destination I particularly cared for

It would have just been a
Temporary anesthetic anyway

I asked New Hope whether
I could be of assistance

They needed someone to assume care for a
Boy recovering from surgery in Hong Kong

He was being cared for by their nurse

If I would relieve her
She could return to her duties

I was Happy to be of Use

When I booked the least expensive flight
I didn't realize it would arrive in Hong Kong
In the middle of the night

Robin booked a night for me at a hotel
They no longer held the tiny flat that
I had stayed with Holly years earlier

I gladly paid out of pocket for my airfare
But felt bad for wasting their funds
Due to my oversight

I checked into the hotel
Exchanged US dollars for Hong Kong dollars

Rested a few hours

Headed to the hospital in the morning

Dignity

The Hong Kong Sanatorium & Hospital is the
Most Prestigious State of the Art Care Center

Private.

The lobby looked more like a grand hotel than a hospital
I checked in at reception to receive directions to the ward

I entered the elevator alone
It was quiet

Sat on my small suitcase
Which held everything I'd need for three weeks

Closed my eyes.

Tired.

But comfortable in my standard San Francisco garb

Flip flops, yoga pants, t-shirt

A few levels up, the doors opened
A well-dressed Woman and her adult Daughter stood waiting

The moment she noticed me
She judged me with Disdain

Scrunched her face as if there was a
Stench in the air

Rolled her eyes
Slight shake of disapproval and annoyance

Leaned to her daughter, scoffed

"Maid from mainland China"

As though it was an

INDIGNITY

To share the same elevator with me

To Instruct me

"Get out!
 You don't belong here!
 Go use the service elevator!"

As she stood with her back to me
I wanted to say in perfect English

"No, Ma'am

I am not a maid from mainland China

I am an Educated American Citizen

On a Mission trip to care for an
Orphaned boy recovering from surgery"

I held my tongue.

There was no point in saying anything to this woman

She didn't care
She wouldn't apologize

She would only scoff at me again
Hold her nose up and irritatingly will the doors to open

Their floor came up and they exited

I was glad for it

Hold On

I found the nurse with John
Behind a curtain in a shared room

She gave me care instructions

As she was preparing to leave

John picked up on it
Began to have separation anxiety

He screamed and cried
Desperately trying to grab the nurse back

She was his only caretaker for weeks

After she left
I tried my best to soothe his pleas

He continued to cry and swat me away

I gave him snacks and ordered lunch
Food. Always a comfort

As I fed him
He realized that I was his one and only now

He calmed down and accepted me
Now he clung to me

Each night
I unfolded a tiny cot to sleep beside his hospital bed

Elite Care

New Hope and MedArt Partner to
Provide the Best Care Possible

Physicians waive their fees
Receive reduced rates with their hospital privileges
Volunteers care for the Children

This Is How Abandoned Children Can

Receive the Same Level of Care From

Esteemed Physicians at a Premier Hospital

Reserved for the Elite

AS THEY SHOULD

Open Hearth

John was about ready to be discharged from the hospital
We needed to stay in Hong Kong to further monitor his condition

He had been battling prolonged infection and wound dehiscence
Still on a foley catheter, along with a persistent cough

Dr. Ngan needed to ensure he was healing properly before fit for travel

It could take a week optimistically
Maybe more

Out of the hospital

We'd have to pay for a hotel
Not a small expense in Hong Kong

Katherine opened her Home to us

We were welcome to stay as long as we needed
Until John was ready to go home

New Blood

Katherine and I went to pick up her daughters from school
Her private driver pulled into the passenger zone

Students casually boarding their private luxury vehicles
Katherine described them as

"Blue Bloods"

An Academy Training the Next Generation of

Blue Bloods of Hong Kong Society and Beyond

although my Education had caught up by now
my bank account did not.

Katherine's friend invited us for dinner

Doris greeted us

Luxury highrise, expansive ocean view, two maids
Huge canary diamond on her hand

I already felt out of place

Katherine was a Corporate Attorney
Doris an MBA Investment Banker

Both Accomplished Women Who
Paused their careers to raise a Family

We brainstormed how We could
Expand New Hope and MedArt's Mission

Fundraising from their Social Circle a Cornerstone
Foster Families a Keystone

Enjoying conversation after dinner

I watched John play amongst
Their daughters with immense curiosity

Big Sisters gave him all their toys

I finally felt Useful again

A Purpose far beyond a paycheck
I really wished I could quit my job

Restart A New Life

A Real Life

Katherine opened her Heart to me
Welcomed me to live with her

Join her Family
A Big Sister to her Girls

She knew plenty of families who would
Compensate well for a private English tutor

I could spend the rest of my time with
New Hope and MedArt

I very much wanted to accept
It seemed like the ideal arrangement

Regrettably

I declined Katherine's generous offer

I didn't think I could fit into Hong Kong Society

In Retrospect

If I could have overcome my own hurdle
I would have done a lot of Good

Fundraise, Expand Networks, Manage Development

Care for Kids, Arrange Foster Families

Coordinate Adoptions

An Endless Priorities List

Katherine and Doris Extended Sincerity

Their Circle of Influence was Great

but I could never be comfortable in a

Society Where People Decide Your Worth

the moment they lay eyes on you

I would not be happy
despite my purposeful intentions

Back home in San Francisco

I breathe freely again
flip flops, yoga pants

I don my hoodie in the brisk wind

2020

We Pushed Full Force to Finality
over petty squabbles

I began to write
This is what I came up with

Revival

I imagine myself in Lost Dynasties
A Girl, disguised as a Boy to enter Academy

To Win the Imperial Exams
To Best All the Boys

First Scholar
First Advisor

Dynasties ruled by Meritocracy are long gone

Dreary Life's Constant

Human Against Human
Aggressor Against Victim

Players Keep Changing
Roles Remain the Same

Existence

Gender, Race, Religion
Country, Politics, Wealth

Man-made fabrications in an
Arbitrary attempt to create Arbitrary Human labels

Groups, Identity, Classification

None of these words truly exist

the way in which these non-existent labels

truly manifests itself is

DIVISION

Knowing Agnostic

I am Agnostic

It would be rather Arrogant of me to
Definitely declare whether

God Exists

Who Is God

Who am I to claim I am all knowing in the Universe?

If God Exists

We Have Got It All Wrong

No True God would dictate Commandments for Us to
Murder and Abuse each other

Too many Atrocities have been committed in the
"Name of God"

Man's Perversion of God's Will to Justify Man's Sin

To Propagandize and Rationalize
His Motivation for Personal Domination

What I can Definitely Declare is that

Any Person Who Claims

They Commit Cruelty

Under the Commandment of God

IS LYING

GAME OVER

To Use Money

As Our Greatest Measure Of Success

Is Our

GREATEST FAILURE

How Does Cyclical Economic Collapse

Not Register As

FAILURE?

Built Into Economic Theory

As If It Was The Natural Order

When You Plan To Fail

YOU FAIL

How Does Extreme Poverty

Not Register As

FAILURE?

We Give Nothing To People

Who Can Afford Nothing

Our Abundance Makes Obvious

Our Waste

Economics

Should Be Built On A

Foundation For Stability

Not Arbitrage.

Arbitrary Rules in a Game

Designed to be Selfish

"May the Best Man Win

I don't care what I Destroy along the way"

"I MUST WIN."

The Worst Men Win Most Often

A Zero-Sum End Pushing Us To Our End

GAME THEORY IS WRONG

Ironic That So Many Nobel Prizes

Have Been Awarded

For This Farce

That Is

Our

FOUNDATIONAL PATHOLOGY

ECONOMICS IS

FOR GIVING

NOT TAKING.

REBOOT

If Life Is A Game

For A Prize Yet To Be Determined

Design The Right Scoreboard

THE GOODY SYSTEM

When You Give
You Win Goody Points

When You Help
You Win Goody Points

Goods and Services Can Be

Freely Exchanged

Free Market

Free Will

Good Is Intrinsic

Not Derived Nor Contrived

Money Is Imaginary

Goody Points Are Real

Goody Points Cannot Be Speculated Nor Hoarded

They hold No Monetary Value outside the system
Nor can You Possibly get them

No One can declare that
Your Moral Bank is suddenly worth less

Just Laugh if They try

"Haha!

Infinite Goody Points!!

Plenty To Go Around For Everyone!!!"

You Cannot Be Morally Bankrupt

Keep Laughing

The Goody System Is A Simple Game

New Game
New Rules

Let's Play

EMPIRICAL PROOF

GOOD WINS

Ladies and Gentlemen

WIN

WIN WIN

Do Not Force People's Will

Win With Sincere Compassion

Free Their Women, Children and Elders

Offer Refuge

Do You think a Mother would choose Loyalty

To a Man who never respected Her
Over the Welfare of Her Family?

NO.
NEVER.

Freed From Oppression And Neglect

She Leads Her Family To Safe Haven

Cowards
Cannot hide behind innocent
Civilian human shields

Ruthless Fighters
Forced to forfeit arms on the battlefield
To farm the fields and cook in the kitchen

Work once toiled by

People They never acknowledged
People Who never asked for war

WIN WIN

WON

Transformers

Life is Simple

Light Water Air Earth

Grape vine capillaries infuse Life into
Mountainous structures climbing skyward

A baseball whizzes through a flurry of
Cherry blossoms swirling over the lush park

Sungold tomato droplets anticipate to pop as your
Impromptu snack on a sunset stroll

Tangles of blackberry thickets define sidewalks

Blueberry pearls collar lamp posts

Hefty apple harvest droops limbs within reach

Breakfast gazing at the warming sky

The morning air brings a waft of honeysuckle

A hummingbird hovers over the coral hibiscus for its first drink of the day

You pluck plump ruby berries

As You

Breathe in the Transformation

HANDS

MARVELOUS TECHNOLOGY

Feed Medicine

Cost Of Healthcare

Is Not Our Barrier To Wellness

POOR DIET IS

The Cost to Feed People Properly is

minuscule compared to the

Consequences of an Improper Diet

Many Ailments Are Not Diseases

They Are Symptoms

Symptoms of a Malnourished Body

Symptoms of an Unfed Mind

Stop Trimming Symptoms

Cure the Root

FOOD IS MEDICINE

Advanced Lifeform

Pharmaceuticals are often artificially extracted to
Produce medications in unnatural dosages

Often with harmful side effects
Unknown consequential dangers

Efficacy is Debatable

We Are Not Evolved To Consume Chemicals

Over hundreds of millions of years
All Lifeforms have proven which sources are beneficial

Wonders We have yet to comprehend
During Our insignificant existence

I dare not suggest all Man-made innovations are inferior

Safe advancements have made
Life-saving treatments affordable and accessible

We Ought To Responsibly

Decode What Nature Provides

OPTIMIZE

NATURAL ADVANCEMENTS

Choose Life

No Mother Would Ever
Willingly Extinguish Life

To Lose a Child is
A Piece of Yourself Forever Gone

She is Fearful

Fear her child will not have a good father
Fear her child will have an abusive father
Fear she cannot provide for her child nor herself
Fear she will be alone in raising her child
Fear she cannot raise her child alone

A DECISION DRIVEN BY FEAR IS

NOT A CHOICE

If She believed she could give her Child a Good Life

SHE WOULD

You cannot leave Mother and Child Destitute
Just so You can stand on higher moral ground

Quell Her Fears

Help Mother Raise Child

Protect Sanctity of Life

Mother and Child

CHOOSE LIFE

Bound Trail

Golden Lotus Feet
A shallow symbol of refined breeding

For Centuries
Crippled feet trapped in a three inch ornate silk slipper

Mothers Require Daughters Subservience in Servitude

A Docile Daughter, a Dutiful Wife, a Doting Mother
To Follow Father, Husband, and Son with Reverent Devotion
To trail far behind Their shadows in Her crippled gait

Men Command

Women Comply
Girls Obey

Subjugation Sold As Morality

A MOTHER IS NOT A MARTYR

STOP WEARING A

HOLLOW BADGE OF HONOR

Bound Fate

Noble and Aristocratic Girls exquisitely wrapped
Presented at the Imperial consort beauty pageantry

Enslaved as playthings in the
Emperor's harem collection

Her Only Utility

To Solidify the Position of a Powerful Family
To Elevate that of a Lesser

Battles in the Harem just as fierce as battles in Court

Her Fate is Bound at Birth

Traded as a Token to Transact Alliances
Forged as a Lure to Seize Power for Her Clan

WHO CAME UP WITH ALL THAT

SHIT !!?!!

Certainly Not The Girl

I couldn't possibly attempt to summarize

Historical and Present

Cruelty on Women

solely to satisfy man's whim

Why Are We Bound?

APATHY

Boundless

My great-grandmother
Gaited on golden lotus feet

She may have been a Daughter
Descended from Affluence and Influence

None of that matters now

What my Ancestors did or didn't do in a past life

In no way makes me inherently better than Anyone

I Still Have To Earn My Position In This Life

BLOODLINE BOUNDS ME TO

NOTHING

NOTHING

BOUNDS ME

Prove It

Men Declare Supremacy Over the Lowly Woman
Based on the Claims

Only Men Can Inherit and Pass Progeny

Woman's Only Utility is to Produce a Male Heir
Otherwise
She is Useless

Men Are Essential

Women Are Disposable

THESE CLAIMS ARE

FACTUALLY

WRONG

False Claim #1

Only Men can inherit and pass bloodline

Refutation #1

Men are easily Cuckolded

Only A Mother Knows She Birthed Her Child

False Claim #2

If a Male Heir cannot be produced
It's the Woman's fault

If a "Useless" Girl is produced
It's the Woman's fault

Refutation #2

Eggs carry only an X Chromosome
Sperm dictates the code for X or Y

XX = Female
XY = Male

If You must be so Inane as to
Assign blame for producing a Girl

SCIENTIFICALLY

MAN FAILS TO SIRE A MALE HEIR

How have we not figured this out for

Millennia ?!?!

Alright,

Maybe #2 could not be verified until
Sex chromosomes were discovered in 1905

But #1?

C'mon

Behold

Ladies

We hold more Power than You know

Man's Most Basic Primal Instinct

Mate and Procreate

He Survives Only Through Us

We Form the World As We Wish Through

Our Progeny

Only Gentlemen Are Fit

We Select for Kindness and Intellect

Not Force of Idiocy

let the unevolved man die out
he decided his own demise

LADIES

WE HOLD ALL THE POWER

Restart

In Anticipation of a Catastrophe of

Our Own Making

We Collect Life to Restart

Man Contributes DNA

Sperm
One of the smallest single living cells in the human body

Produced in trillions over His Lifetime

Woman Contributes DNA

An Egg, the largest single living cell in the Human Body

An Egg created while in Her Mother's Womb

An Egg which cannot be Regenerated

An Egg She's carried all Her Life

This Egg

She Gives to Man

HUMANITY'S VESSEL

if man fails to adapt

he can end in one of two ways

Finality

Women Die, except One

Men Survive

Man Harms Woman

He Kills the Last Woman

desperate.

Man attempts to grow Life in an artificial environment

you can't.

Man Regrets.

He lives Every Day to his Dying Day in Regret

Regret He did not cherish every Woman

Regret He hurt Woman

Regret Gentleman

FAILED

To Protect Woman

woman dies

woman's egg dies

last wisp of man's hope dies

man's final extinction.

We Gift You Life

How Can You Possibly Fail To Appreciate Us?

Rebirth

Men Die, except One

Women Survive

The Last Man dies naturally

in nine months

Woman Births

A New Species of

Global Citizens

Raised By Amazonian Women

Natural Selection

Intelligent Design

Nurture Selected Nature

WOMAN

EVOLVES

MAN

Ladies

Reserve Your Sacred Egg

Only For The Deserved Gentleman

Heaven on Earth

Heaven is an Infinite maze of halls
Each door holds Secrets to the Universe

To Gleefully run through these halls for Eternity

To Peek into each door
Sometimes to Step through

With each Lesson
A Multitude of New Doors Unlock

My Idea of Heaven

LET US

CONSTRUCT IT NOW

Providence

Provide For Every Person

Food   Shelter   Medicine

EDUCATION

Every Person Can Live Their Best Life

A FAIR GAME

OPEN PORTAL

We Unlock the

Global Consciousness of

Infinite Human Potential

We Unlock

Secrets of the Universe

WE UNLOCK

NOW

Idealist

All My Life

my parents have vehemently criticized me

"You are Too Idealistic !!!

You always want to be the Best !!

You want everything to be Perfect !!"

"The World Is Not Perfect !!!

You Can't Expect It To Be !!!!!"

why not?

my parents never even possibly suggested that
I could accomplish whatever I set my heart on

only to tell me that I was

FOOLISH

for even thinking so

they don't know me
they underestimate me

the agony.

I just don't let it bother me as much anymore

A friend once tried to comfort me

"Jenny
 You are Smart.

 You are So Smart
 Your Parents don't know what to do with you"

I'm beginning to see that now

THEY WERE WRONG

an unfulfilled idealist is

Agony

AN IDEALIST

WITH THE MEANS IS

FORMIDABLE

Untamable

Intellect Should Never Be Stifled

Greatness Is Not Easy

Taking It Easy Is Not So Great

my mother has been trying to
tame me my whole life

sorry, mom

I must run Wild

Write Awake

For decades
I have had a recurring dream

In this dream
I have Won the Nobel Peace Prize

Before the World
I take this Prize

Kneel before my Mother
Give it to her

while in the dream
it feels so real, tangible

within my grasp

Suddenly I wake

Awake
The dream feels distant, unobtainable
I pinch myself for such a silly fantasy

Wide Awake
I wonder what I, an ordinary girl could
Accomplish Worthy of a Nobel Prize

As I Write
I feel this dream drifting toward me

awake or asleep

we live in a dreamlike state

a reality of our own construction

IRREFUTABLE PROOF

I am no ordinary girl
I am a Girl with an Extraordinary Job to Finish

I WANT EVERY ACCOLADE

Not for my personal glory
For the Greater My Influence

THE LOUDER

MY MESSAGE RESONATES

I am Jenny

I am a Girl

You Mandated My Death In The Womb

You Would Have Murdered Me At Birth

You Deemed My Life Unworthy

I am here to tell You

THIS IS WHAT

A GIRL

CAN DO

A GIRL

DESERVES

TO LIVE

I Was Born To Prove This

World Peace

You each hold a slip of paper in your hand
Contemplate Your Purpose in this Life

Day after day, year after year
You grasp this slip

Did You Live Out Your Purpose?

I hope Your two words are the same as Mine

Hurry

They are waiting for Us

This Is My Best Shot

The First Shot

Men Wrote the Book Completely Wrong

Since the Dawn of Civilization

Ladies and Gentlemen

LET US

REWRITE

there exists only one key

that unlocks secrets of the universe

believe in what a girl can do

thank you for reading my tale

I invite You to write along

Our Shared Journey

ready to turn the world upside down?

Right Side Up

the ship is launching

are you in or out?

勇媽

Mothers Lead

Jenny Athena Wong

A Memoir

A Modern Woman

A Mission

一個女人的日記

The Journey of a Girl to Motherhood

The Power of Women to Advance Evolution

The Mission to Empower Women
Who Will In Turn
Elevate All

勇媽

Mothers Lead™

Jenny Athena Wong©

In sharing my Life Story
I laid bare my Soul
For Your Sake

I only ask for Reciprocal Respect
For the Memory of My Companions
On this Journey thus far

here comes the boring stuff
I tried to protect you by placing it in the back

mumble jumble required verbiage and such

please forgive me.

forgiven?